Dedications & Other Darkhorses

Lost in the Bonewheel Factory

Copacetic

I Apologize for the Eyes in My Head

Toys in a Field

Dien Cai Dau

February in Sydney

Magic City

Neon Vernacular: New and Selected Poems

Thieves of Paradise

Blue Notes: Essays, Interviews and Commentaries

Pleasure Dome: New and Collected Poems

Talking Dirty to the Gods

TABOO

TABOO

THE WISHBONE TRILOGY

PART ONE

YUSEF KOMUNYAKAA

FARRAR, STRAUS AND GIROUX / NEW YORK

FARRAR, STRAUS AND GIROUX
19 Union Square West, New York 10003

Distributed in Canada by Douglas & McIntyre Ltd.
Printed in the United States of America
FIRST EDITION, 2004

Grateful acknowledgment is made to the following publications and
anthologies, in which some of these poems originally appeared: *Agni*;
The American Poetry Review; *Black Warrior Review*; *Boston Review*; *Brilliant
Corners*; *Callaloo*; *The Columbia Review*; *Field*; *The Georgia Review*; *The
Iowa Review*; *The Kenyon Review*; *The Lincoln Theater Center Review*; *Poetry
East*; *Poetry London*; *The Southern California Anthology*; *Urbanus*; *The Best
American Poetry 1995, 1996, 1997*; *The Body Electric*; *Poets of the Next
Century*; *The Second Set*; and *Uncommonplace: An Anthology of Contemporary
Louisiana Poets.* "Lament and Praise Song" was the 1998 Harvard Phi Beta
Kappa poem.

Library of Congress Cataloging-in-Publication Data
Komunyakaa, Yusef.
    Taboo / Yusef Komunyakaa.— 1st ed.
        p.   cm. — (The wishbone trilogy ; pt. 1)
Includes bibliographical references.
    ISBN-13: 978-0-374-29148-8
    ISBN-10: 0-374-29148-9 (hardcover : alk. paper)
    1. Blacks—Poetry.   I. Title.

PS3561.O455T33 2004
811'.54—dc22
                                        2003026176

Designed by Gretchen Achilles

www.fsgbooks.com

10   9   8   7   6   5   4   3   2   1

TO THE MEMORY OF JEHAN,

REETIKA, AND ZOE

CONTENTS

LINGO   3

IMHOTEP   6

AGHRIBAT AL-ARAB   8

HENRY THE NAVIGATOR   11

OTHER WORLDS   13

BACCHANAL   14

ASTRAEA'S FOOTNOTES   16

QUEEN MARIE-THÉRÈSE & NABO   18

LAMENT & PRAISE SONG   21

SUNSET IN SURINAM   24

MONTICELLO   27

UNFRAMING A TRIPTYCH   29

CAPTAIN AMASA DELANO'S DILEMMA   32

BEFORE THE WINDOWS   35

DOUBLE EXPOSURE   37

KING OF THE OCTAVE   39

THE PRICE OF BLOOD   42

THE QUADROON'S MASQUE BALL   44

ANTEBELLUM SILHOUETTES   47

TOBE'S BLUES   51

OTHELLO'S ROBE   55

JEANNE DUVAL'S CONFESSION   58

HAGAR'S DAUGHTER   61

CHIAROSCURO	66
NUDE STUDY	68
TRUEBLOOD'S BLUES	69
SATCHMO, USA	71
CANTE JONDO	75
THE HOUSE	78
TO BEAUTY	80
DADDY RED	82
TWILIGHT SEDUCTION	84
HOMAGE TO A BELLHOP	88
FORGIVE & LIVE	91
SÉANCE & SHADOWPLAY	94
LUSTRATION	97
LUCUMI	99
OIL	102
AT THE RED SEA	105
IN LINE AT THE BANK	108
TROUBLING THE WATER	110
NETHERWORLDS	113
LINGUA FRANCA	117
THE ARCHIVIST	119
DESECRATION	127
OUTSIDE THE BLUE NILE	129

TABOO

Herodotus, woven into his story,
   tells how the Phoenicians lent
      war fleets to Greece & Egypt,

how a ghost-driven flotilla
   eased like salmon up birth water
      & sailed the Red Sea,

hoping to circumnavigate Africa
   around the Cape of Good Hope
      & along Gibraltar. A blue

door opened. Diodorus
   says of the Ethiopians,
      "born under the Sun's path,"

that "its warmth may have ripened them
   earlier than other men." As if
      a ventriloquist inherited

the banter of a sailor's parrot,
   words weave with Herodotus's —
      angel food . . . sellers didn't touch

the gold . . . devil's food. The stories
   become flesh as these ghosts
      argue about what's lost

in translation, believing two images
   should spawn & ignite a star
      in the eyes of a sphinx

or soothsayer. Sometimes they do.
    There's a reason why the dead
        may talk through a medium

about how Aryans drove cattle
    along the seven rivers & left
        dark-skinned Dravidians

with tongues cut out, sugarcane
    fields ablaze, & the holy air
        smelling of ghee & soma.

These ghosts know the power
    of suggestion is more than body
        language: white list, black

sheep, white tie, black market.
    Fear climbs the tribal brainstem
        or wills itself up an apple tree,

hiding from the dream animal
    inside. The serpent speaks
        like a Lacan signifier,

posing as a born-again agrarian
    who loves computer terminals
        better than cotton blossoms

planted, then we wail to reap
    whirlwind & blessing. Each prefix
        clings like a hookworm

inside us. If not the split-tongued
  rook, the sparrow is condemned
     to sing the angel down.

IMHOTEP

His forehead was stamped, *Administrator*
   of the Great Mansion. Unloved in the
      Crescent City, I sat in a bathtub

clutching a straight razor.
   Desire had sealed my mouth
      with her name. I asked,

What do full moons & secret herbs
   have to do with a man's heartache?
      But this sage from the island of Philae

just smiled. Here before me stood the Son
   of Ptah. Dung beetles & amethyst . . .
      cures for a mooncalf,

flaccidity, bad kidneys, gout,
   & gallstones. What we knew
      about the blood's map

went back to the court
   of King Zoser. Something
      beneath this April dream

scored by voices passing
   outside my front door, a rap song
      thundering from a boogie box.

I wasn't dead. This Homeric healer
   from the Serapeum of Memphis
      lingered in the room.

I folded the bright blade
   back into its mother-of-pearl
      handle, & laughed at the noise

in the street, at a yellow moth
   beating wings into dust
      against a windowpane.

At the party, Omar
    & Sally, the three
        of us deconstruct

& reassemble Oklahoma City,
    between shots of tequila
        as Hassan's *qarqba*

shrinks the room into a big
    talking drum. Snowflakes
        pelt the windows till

I drift in a sandstorm
    that drives us across
        hidden centuries

to those black poets
    known as the Crows
        of the Arabs before

Islam in Arabia.
    They were all unnamed
        by patriarchs, their mothers

Ethiopian concubines.
    If we say 'Antara,
        echoes will whisper,

"The Suspended Odes,
    the seven *Mu'allaqat*,
        & his father's tribe

was 'Aba & his mother
   was called Zabiba."
      They know of his love

for his cousin 'Abla
   who snubbed him,
      & can tell the day

& hour when the 'Aba
   lost a battle & what
      he said to his father:

" 'Antara is a slave,
   & he does not know
      how to charge—

only to milk camels
   & bind their udders."
      They say his sword

bloodied the dunes
   when he was freed,
      & he called his mother

"the hyena that thrives
   on an abandoned camp,
      legs of an ostrich . . . "

They'll speak of Khufaf
   next: the tribe's chief,
      also called Ibn Nadba

after his mother."
   Of course, nobody talks
      about Suhaym (Habba),

the Nubian servant
   who seduced the women,
      saying that "prison

is no more than a
   shadow of the house
      I live in, a whipping

no more than hide
   meeting hide." Omar
      sucks the pale worm

from the tequila bottle,
   caught in the icy glow
      of the windowpanes.

As Sally leans forward
   for me to light her
      cigarette, I cup

the flame in my hands,
   thinking how the men burned
      Suhaym, that the women

said they were crying
   only for dead stars
      falling into the Red Sea.

He dreamt of latitude, his mind
   on constellations & astrolabes,
     some maritime lodestar

jostling the magnetic field
   & mystifying the sextant,
     pulling him beyond

the sight of land. Caravels,
   piled with a mapmaker's desire
     & atlases blessed by God,

he pushed on till they could
   taste the salty luster
     of precious metals,

till the sea vultures
   turned around at midday
     to backtrack their hunger

to Portugal. The seamen
   spoke to the sky & crossed
     themselves. Gold drew

the ships onward, to where
   twilight turned into an anchor
     against a bruised horizon

& the towering sails cast
   shapes of monsters across
     a grassy dawn, to where

the day looked like two hundred
    & thirty-five silhouettes
        tied to the ground

& no prayers or tallow lanterns
    could grubstake enough light
        to the brain's dark continent.

Hair & skin damp with holy water
    & blood, we slouched to the Algarve
        yoked like dust-colored oxen,

their dreams etched into ours
    on trampled paths as far north
        as Lisbon. We made love

& died to transfuse Spain & Portugal.
    Ringed inside like grandfather trees,
        names tumored under new languages

as wide-hipped women stole voices
    out of lusty soil. We worked
        the fields, followed the sun

as stevedores, & mastered curses—
    Estevanico & Alonzo beside Cortés,
        Pizarro, Balboa, Menéndez,

& de Soto—trekked virgin forests
    to force blood to sing forbidden
        oaths, to outrun sugar & indigo.

BACCHANAL

Rubens paints desire
  in his wife's eyes
    gazing up at the black man

who has an arm around
  her waist. Tambourines
    shake the dusky air alive,

& there's a hint of tulips,
  a boy touching his penis
    at the edge of jubilation.

Has a war been won, have dogs
  been driven from the gates,
    or the old fattened calf

slaughtered? Cartwheels
  tie one Pan-hoofed season
    to the next, with Bacchus

& Zulus. We believe
  there's pure quartz
    hidden in this room

fretting the light,
  forcing hands to reach
    for each other, beyond

ambrosia. His wife
  seduced by joy & unction,
    wants to know how long

he's danced with a brush
   to will the night's hunger
      into an orgasm of colors.

After spying at Antwerp
  for Charles II, Aphra Behn
    sang of tropic Surinam

over winter stones for warmth
  in a debtors' prison. But
    this wasn't where *Oroonoko*

first rolled off the tongue
  as if she'd rehearsed it
    for years in her spleen.

The tale, a faction, a lyric
  saga in a pale throat—
    a woman who pawned her rings

& dared to endow a black man
  with nobility & gallantry
    in a thicket of thieves

& scalawags. The gallery
  of voices called, "Sappho
    famous for her gout

& guilt." She gave her hero
  a mind. Did someone think
    that next she'd whisper,

"fabulous Priapus,"
  as she penned his name?
    Drops of rain throbbed

on a lily. They pranced
   out secondhand effigies
      of harlot & sluggard

to diminish her talent
   & wit beneath footprints.
      Because this daughter

of a barber & a wet nurse
   could not heal herself
      with gifts of Indian

feathers & butterflies,
   but only with flesh itself,
      she was a satirist's envoi:

"Poverty, poetry, pox,
   are plagues enough for one."
      Those louts tried to steal

her image & whittle it
   down to a mutable footnote,
      to a blade of lye soap

they bathed with till
   it was a sliver of regret,
      not even half as noble

as Oroonoko, who stood
   in a forest to behead
      his beloved & cover her with petals.

When Duquesne presented
   the Queen with a dwarf
      from Dahomey named Nabo,

another scandal strolled
   into the palace. At first
      he was there to show off

her alabaster skin
   & carry her train.
      She would dress him

in silk robes, bejeweled
   bracelets & armbands,
      a turban which sparkled

with an aigrette
   of rubies & pearls
      given by Madame de Maintenon.

He was the only one
   who entered Her Majesty's boudoir
      before she was out of bed,

& his wit sent plumes
   of laughter into the cold
      morning air. As she dined

on chocolates, the fat
   shook on her royal bones,
      her skin like rice paper.

Maybe moonlight
   ravaged the room
      when she invited him

into her bed, as she
   spoke about eating
      green fruit & live birds

in her dreams; mystery—
   when the Queen birthed
      a daughter, Nabo

was already days dead.
   The doctors kept
      telling the King,

"The color of the child
   was caused by a black man
      looking at the Queen."

The horse hooves
   struck sparks from stone
      as the royal carriage

rounded a hairpin curve
   in the road, hurrying
      a secret to the convent

of Moret. Years later,
   Voltaire said the Black Nun
      was the King's daughter,

but Le Nôtre says,
 "Would the Queen, Marie-
  Thérèse, the Dauphin,

the Duke & the Duchess
 of Bourgogne, have shown
  the same attachment

to her?" If you stand
 before her portrait
  at the Library of St. Geneviève

for fifteen minutes,
 gazing at the bottom
  of chance & requital,

the vigil of her father's
 eyes, you'll see everything
  known about love & death.

At this hour of unlettered
   clocks, ghosts of Milton & Pope
      gaze at one of my first loves

as she writes *An Ethiop tells you*
   to the students of the University
      of Cambridge. We were teenagers

when I fell for her
   portrait of composure
      crosshatched like tribal marks

on an oval frontispiece: Phillis
   Wheatley, Negro Servant
      to Mr. John Wheatley,

of Boston. At this hour
   of wounded second hands,
      I say what I think

she'd say to you: Please
   follow imagination like a lover
      into the eardrum & inner

sanctum, into the secret rooms
   behind seven chambers of naked
      doubt. Here, now, this

anecdotal green & fretwork
   hide trees she strolled past,
      but I know of no shortcuts

to bypass the run-down
   boardinghouse where she
      scrubbed & polished floors.

We don't have to walk
   out of our bodies to go
      there, because clocks & bells

sway in towers of glass
   & mortar to transport us
      in the hull of a ship

of stormy midnights
   in the belly of Moby Dick
      where she crouched inside

seven years of African
   memory. At this hour
      among canonical roses

with seditious thorns,
   I wonder if the tongues
      of that tribunal of good men

quizzing her turned to dust
   in pure Latin & Greek.
      We are blessed if we can see her

on the streets of Cambridge,
   in her heroic couplets,
      rescued by our imagination:

a faint perfume of England
    nestles in Puritan cloth
        when she shakes the hand

of George Washington,
    & clocks of pewter strike
        till new leaves redden the quad.

Blake's worktable was lit
  by an imaginary sunset
    as he crosshatched

scenes from Stedman's head
  onto copper plates.
    A gallery of flogged

bodies hung in midair,
  strung between words
    & deeds of this officer

in the Scots Brigade,
  his initials stamped
    on a woman's hip. *Aboma*

Snake, Flagellation,
  & Gallows. Joanna,
    the daughter of Kruythoff

& a slave called Cery,
  was a refrain whispered
    as she stood between him

& hell. At fifteen,
  she calmed his fever
    & ferried him back

to a cerulean horizon.
  Drums on a May hill ignited
    the morning they married.

By October, when she
        was sold to Passalage
            & Son, he hadn't touched her

for five hard months,
        afraid that a child
            would make her worth

more. He languished
        between one lonely idea
            & another. Neptune,

the slave *broken alive*
        upon the rack, was less
            than a wisp of smoke

overtaking him in blond
        sage. Maybe it was
            a day like no other,

a bloated hush-filled
        sanctuary *like the roes*
            in the forest that created

their son. Jack.
        He tried to outrun
            cries of guinea fowl,

but the sun on brass
        buttons & insignias
            followed him to Tiverton

in Devon. The mermaid
   he courted in daydreams
      was the same Joanna

sold to a Mrs. Godefoy,
   who said she was poisoned
      by pity's belladonna.

Beverly, Harriet, Madison,
  Eston, all with sandy red hair
    & listed in Jefferson's *Farm*

Book. The deepest doors
  open in soil & flesh, rooms
    designed to lead into others

& alcoves where a kiss
  is stolen. His fingers
    flashed through chenille,

Virginia rails into November
  afternoons. Their wet sighs
    seethed into poems by Thomas

Moore, & William Cullen Bryant.
  Black Sal, Monticellan Sally,
    a ditty sung to Yankee

Doodle. This dome-shaped
  room, did they kiss & hug
    here, gazing out over

luteous fields as round windows
  changed the world? Did lies
    coagulate on the roof

of the mouth like stalactites
  of blood? This architect,
    a central protagonist

in passion, tiptoed & turned
   doorknobs after midnight.
      Are cries of blame & joy

still spiraling around
   the aurora borealis?
      Words: *I advance it,*

therefore, as a suspicion
   only, that the blacks . . .
      are inferior to the whites

in the endowment of body
   & mind. As he talked & dined,
      did the women ever face

each other like Philomela
   & Procne, a nightingale
      & swallow, on a forked

branch in their minds? If
   we try hard enough, he's still
      at his Neoclassical desk

musing, but we know his mind
   is brushing aside abstractions
      so his hands can touch flesh.

One color divides
   into another like the dark
      eyes of Marie Dumas,

into the Marquis de la
   Pailleterie's night song
      in the overworked, leached out

red hills of Haiti.
   The watercolorist
      says how hard it is

to tame a dream's
   wild borders. Unbelievable
      feats of their offspring:

three duels in one day,
   thirteen soldiers captured
      single-handed, "La Légion

Americaine," Eastern
   Pyrenees, Mont Cenis,
      "Horatius Cocles of the Tyrol"—

the general's blood seethed
   into the son's prolific pen.
      Images of D'Artagnan

sprouted from the father
   as if from Zeus's head,
      & somehow somewhere

when Napoleon said,
  "Good morning, Hercules—
    you have beaten the hydra"

he was talking to Alexandre,
  fils, père. The friend
    of poachers—600 glasses

of absinthe won at a bar,
  & creator of *Christine,*
    The Three Musketeers,

The Black Tulip—
  Chevalier de Maison
    Rouge written in sixty-six

hours on a bet. Did gold
  coins stacked on a table
    belong to all three,

& which one said what
  to Roger de Beauvoir
    about his wife, Ida

Ferrier? Whose fingers
  slipped coins into the other's
    vest pockets? In this

triptych we can't
  untie the fine gestures,
    can't say where one

line severs another.
  To cut one image
    out of the frame

without damaging the rest,
  you must prick a thumb
    with an X-Acto knife

because only blood can
  loosen the glue & secrets
    holding this deed together.

The day the albatross
   colored the sky with shit,
      I stumbled upon Benito

Cereno's pirate ship
   tarrying on the high seas.
      A ramrod Spanish sailor

locked eyes with me
   & gestured at the hot sky
      with his marlinspike.

But I wasn't a reader
   of Freemason signs
      or symbols of modern

oblivion. The motley lot
   sat on the quarterdeck
      dragging down the sun

to polish their hatchets,
   & it was as if God
      conspired with them

so I couldn't see
   through their percussion.
      That old sea salt

who handed me the wet
   Gordian knot to undo,
      his words were lost

because Cereno stole
   my mind with a litany
      of silent signs,

though I mastered
   satire & irony
      a lifetime ago.

I would have sat
   in the captain's chair
      & said, "Shave me,

Nigger." To me, Babo
   could only have been a body
      servant. Those sphinx

shadows posted as lookouts
   & lieutenants of the plot,
      they were only the malingerers

to me. The cries of babies
   leapt from my groin
      when I saw the negress

slumbering like a mermaid
   on a rock. How was I to know
      this wasn't the season myths

sang flesh & blood
   to sleep? That bastard,
      their headsman, Babo,

his skull was a hive
     we had to nail to a pole
          in the plaza as a warning

to ourselves. They say
     I didn't master the beast
          inside my own noggin,

but I want the naysayers
     to know I am the corpus
          of unquestionable deeds

before my conception,
     before I kicked against
          the walls of the womb,

& my unblinking eyes
     weren't gazing toward
          a monastery on Mt. Agonia.

Some would like to think morphine,
    ether, & those un-English
    afternoons in Florence

stole one hundred love sonnets
    from Elizabeth Barrett Browning;
    or that it began with "Bro"

drowning off Torquay.
    Maybe a word or look
        from Harriet Beecher Stowe

picked the lock on a door
    small as a locket.
        Some believe "The Runaway

Slave at Pilgrim's Point" didn't
    begin on the estate at Durham,
        Herefordshire, that the words

couldn't have been etched alongside
    "Prometheus Bound," & an oath
        hidden & sung beneath breath

transfused her at 50 Wimpole Street.
    That it was the sunlight in France
    & Italy igniting till tropic

blooms opened an unnamed night
    beneath an invalid's white skin:
        I am not mad: I am black.

Some would like to think
    Elizabeth was purely English.
      But a scorpion & angel

stole part of her before
    the window of Casa Guidi
      cast her bones into a lamp.

When wing-footed Perseus
  wore his midnight helmet
    to slay the Gorgons

& behead Medusa
  the gods were pleased.
    Sometimes mortals talk

themselves into earthly sky.
  Queen Cassiopeia boasted
    she was more beautiful

than the daughters of Nereus.
  But the gods grew vengeful
    & demanded her daughter

sacrificed to a serpent.
  The Ethiopians were devoured
    by the hundreds, till

the girl's father, Cepheus,
  said, Yes. Andromeda
    lay chained to a rocky ledge

beside the rough sea,
  & agile Perseus fell
    in love with her. After

he slew the sea serpent
  they sailed to Greece,
    to a place between body

& mind. In another time,
over two thousand years
away, I laugh, thumbing

pages of photographs
on the history of rock
& roll: black & white

dancers sway to rhythm
& blues, separated by a rope
down the center of the club.

Praise made me lonely
    for Cuban plantain, mango,
        & papaya. I won first place

in violin at ten. After
    France's Legion of Honor
        & Order of the Black Eagle

in Berlin, I received
    my German citizenship
        & married a noblewoman.

But I couldn't stay
    in one place. I tell you,
        myths & lies tailed me.

In Mexico City
    I rented the best hotel room,
        & they say I left it a shambles.

I don't remember saying it was
    "a remembrance of having been in
    the land of the hidalgos."

I do remember this: a rich miner
    asked me to play at a soiree
        for 800 francs in gold.

I hadn't eaten for a day,
    & I don't know why I insisted
        he pay me 1000 francs.

That night, I played
    till notes swelled the mansion.
    I could have taken any one

of those lovesick daughters
    as I glided under a drunken sky
    before they could thank me.

I never felt sorry
    for myself. My flesh
        & blood back in Germany,

their voices were always
    in my violin. But it took rum
        & tuberculosis to slow me

down. Somebody found me
    in a hovel in Buenos Aires,
        as if I were a ghost

born to dog Mengele
    on walks. My children,
        holding their bows,

were they sterilized alongside
    those "Rhineland bastards"
        fathered by black Frenchmen?

When the medical students
    raised me onto a slab
        between a thief & a suicide,

I taunted them. The souvenir
in my tattered vest pocket
was an embossed riddle,

but Chevalier de Brindis
Baron de Sala was the name
on my German passport.

They asked, Who is this
corseted like a gentleman
under a vagabond's clothes?

THE PRICE OF BLOOD

—AFTER T. S. NOBLE'S PAINTING

The planter's son now hates
  the part of himself he loved
    more than anything.

You can see the faded image
  of the Sacrifice of Isaac
    bleeding through.

A mockingbird mimics betrayal,
    & now there's money for gifts.
      Maybe the son's thinking

of what Aesop said to Xanthus
  about the caged bird. Aloof,
    with one hand on his hip,

he's cocky as his mother.
    Pyramids of gold on the table
      balance out the scene.

Holding the bill of sale
  in his hand, the slave trader
    could be a circuit judge,

a preacher, an undertaker.
    The planter's averted eyes
      take us to Colonel Tom

dead on the floor in Langston's
    Mulatto. Cora argues with God
      beneath a chinaberry tree

with her head bowed, gazing
  at a sign in the dust: Aurora's
    grasshopper on an anthill.

Where's the wife,
  in the parlor listening
    to their daughter play

Schumann's "Auf einer Burg"
  so lightly it seethes through
    the walls? The son flinches

& puffs up his chest like a banty
  rooster, trying not to cry
    as he holds back the sun.

I tell a servant
   to wrap me in a carpet
      as a gift for Caesar.

Quadrilles & the clank
   of keys for houses
      on St. Ann Street—

I recite Mme. du Deffand's
   letters to my protector
      scented with absinthe.

I am the daughter
   of a creole & concubine,
      whose gilded barge

sails the river Cydnus
   with boys dressed as Cupid
      fanning me. Purple

incense drifts to both
   sides of the bank. Brutus
      is dead at Philippi,

& I stand in the Virgin
   Mother Isis's translucent
      robe, dissolving a pearl

in a goblet for Antony.
   This barge is a ballroom's
      dazzle on the Mississippi

as I dance a silhouette
    between worlds. One bead
        of blood leads to the next

oath & plumed helmet,
    & the day arrives when Antony
        is lowered into my tomb

to die in my arms.
    Africa haunts my blood
        till my body remembers

the ship's sway & groan.
    Octavius stands in my bedroom
        saying he'll kill my children

if I drink the poison.
    Playing my role, I mask
        so others cannot see

themselves. I promise
    I won't cry when he
        goes home to his wife.

One maid dresses me in silk
    & jewels. Another hands me
        the sweetest fruit. Now,

I am Queen of Earth,
    of Egypt, sitting here
        on St. Ann, with a crown

& scepter, as I lift a coiled
   asp from a basket of figs
      & hold it to my left breast.

. . . and that this penalty of death
was dealt them by their own husband
or father or brother as the case might be.
—LILLIAN SMITH, *KILLERS OF THE DREAM*

The war's over. Daddy's dead
    beneath a hero's white oak,
        & I'm left with this

gimpy leg, a Yankee's
    bullet nestled in a bone
        finer than Grecian

porcelain. The cotton flowers
    are gone. Voices stolen
        from the air, days

left like mud eels
    after the river's receded—
        gone up north & down

to the devil. Carpetbaggers
    everywhere, talking out of both
        sides of their mouths

& putting puppet niggers
    in high places. Dixie's
        in the canebrake

like a corn-shuck doll.
    Mother's dressed up
        in lace & taffeta,

sitting upstairs, playing
    solitaire. The silos are empty,
        & the fields bound

with come-along vines & kudzu.
    Is it any wonder I drink moonshine?
        Yes, now, this damn burden

passed down from father
    to son, in the blood's
        first howl from cave

to Stonehenge, this
    scalawag's oath & naked
        privilege. Can I

do it? Daddy would have
    if he'd seen only half
        of what I've witnessed.

He would have killed
    them both by now. If
        Sister is so smart,

doesn't she know Big Carl
    is Daddy's bastard son?
        Good God, what am I

saying? The house niggers
    laugh behind their hands.
        When I first came back

I held my sister
        in my arms, but couldn't stop
        trembling. She wasn't

a little girl anymore.
        Everything here was sad
        except her. The fields

languished between yellow
        & brown. The corn mash
        better than ever;

its old bite just as deep.
        Someone was there
        like a ghost

from the battlefields—
        she stood in the room
        peering at me. Nude

beneath lamp-lit
        cloth. Did she think
        I was drunk?

I saw her
        ease down the stairs
        & out the side door.

Big Carl's shadow
        was tall as the oak
        they stood beneath;

his arms around her waist
  & her moving against him
    as if to climb a hill

or swim upstream. They won't be
  laughing behind their hands
    when a horse bucks

& her right foot tangles
  in the runaway's stirrup—
    when she trips

on the top step
  & falls to the bottom
    with a broken neck,

& me there rocking
  her back & forth
    in my drunken arms.

I walked into that house
   with its blue-slate
      spires & cupolas,

went there with iron
   in my body, when sunlight
      still played Miss Emily

like piney-wood fingers
   on a banjo. I heard
      with half the white men

dead after the War,
   some plantation women
      moved black overseers

into their houses . . .
   Anyway, Colonel Sartoris
      still spoke to her

nightly. Don't care
   how many rooms in a house,
      it can turn into a sand castle

with winds off the Gulf.
   Not even a radio tuned
      to Jackson, Homer Barron's

smile worked like a skeleton key.
   I can't say how many times
      I shook his yellow gloves

from my shoulders.
 I was young, she was
  young, but I never spent

a night in that place,
 except when she was sick
  three years ago. Some days,

when I first came there,
 our shadows hid under beds
  & behind doors. Sometimes

we'd walk miles around
 each other in that old house.
  No, I can't say her lavender

never stole my breath,
 that we never placed a hand
  over the other's mouth.

Women shook their heads
 when I'd stroll past
  with my market basket.

I told that emotional
 carperbagger if he didn't
  underline his P's & Q's,

something would happen.
 Sometimes the outside
  can't match the inside.

The doors & windows sag,
   & it isn't because something
      within or underneath

surrenders. I promised her
   I'd never repeat or try
      to sing the nightbird's vow.

I nailed shut the door
   to her bedroom, knowing
      they'd hammer it open

soon as she was in earth.
   I know them, the weak points
      & where the studs embrace

to hold evening sky up.
   If sparrows didn't hide
      in the attic, I'd be myself

again, wrestling oak
   & pine. Getting used
      to strong light again.

But nothing as bright
   as Miss Emily's China
      painting she hoped to break

Homer Barron's spell
   with. I can't count the days
      those twenty-five-cent pieces

meant hocks in the beans.
   The scent of yellow roses
      isn't all that keeps her

here. I'm in these woods
   because I have a tongue
      & thorns burn my fingers.

OTHELLO'S ROBE

This is pure velvet,
   darned with strands
     of maiden hair,

the hem & sleeves
   frayed a bit. Years
     ago, when an admirer

sent it with an embossed
   certificate of authenticity,
     I wonder if she knew

she snared me in colors
   bright as Joseph's coat.
     All these towns along

the eastern seaboard
   & through the Midwest,
     this damn robe's kept me

moving as if bloodhounds
   dogged my trail. Sweetheart,
     I must add your perfume

to this concoction
   stealing my senses. After
     each curtain call you sit

in my lap, hugging
   roses to your breasts,
     in the arms of Ira Aldridge

at the Theatre Royal
    in a gold-leafed room,
        riding the fantasy wheel

to its true mark.
    The African Roscius.
        Into my left sleeve

I tucked a woman's lace
    handkerchief & a letter
        from Sir Edmund Kean.

Born on Greene Street,
    New York City, I arrived
        in Liverpool as the yes-man

of James Wallack. After
    Shylock & Lear, it was still
        hard to keep my head

when Queen Adelaide
    awarded me the Verdienst
        Gold Medal. Forget

what Théophile Gautier
    said in St. Petersburg.
        As we travel from Boise

to Spokane, I hurt
    for Tolstoy's wit
        & Shevchenko's metaphors;

I hunger for the old days
in Europe when they wanted
to drag Iago off the stage

& thrash him good. Now
they only come to flesh
out fears, & I can't help

but desire to wield a dagger
that doesn't have a spring
buried in a rhinestone handle.

Because Charles couldn't
   dare beyond my breasts
     & berry-colored lips

saying, "Madame est
   servie" in a short play,
     I never stopped seeing him

as some bouffant boy,
   with an armload of roses
     outside that stage door,

petals in Paris snow.
   Locked in his Babel
     of books, he quizzed himself

till he was nothing
   but a diseased root,
     till I was a whore

& Black Madonna,
   not an actual woman
     beneath conjured cloth

& sheer lackluster.
   It wasn't my idea
     to garnish an apartment

with a blond maid.
   I became Beatrice
     & Hamlet's mother,

seduced with tropic fruit
between a lion's den
& paradise. A bemused

lament, a brown body,
a good luck charm
found on Friday

the thirteenth. "Obi,
Faustus . . . ebony thighs,
child of midnight. . . ."

Charles tried to work me
out of his heart & spleen,
but I'd been made into

a holy wild perfume,
a vertigo of bells in his head,
the oboe's mouth-hole

licked with opium.
A Haitian cock bristled
beneath my shoulder blades,

& only gold coins
could calm me down.
The most precious litany

dripped from his melancholy
quill. Even his red-haired
beggar girl possessed

my breasts. Charles
    was hexed from head to toe,
        but it wasn't my fault.

His mother said she
    burned my letters because
        I never said I loved

her son. He tried
    to erase what he'd created
        by mouthing Latin verses

beneath Wagner's piano.
    As I leaned in an alley
        on my crutches, behind

a pie shop, halfway
    to a pauper's grave, it was
        then he stole a last breath

because I couldn't stop
    saying how much I loved
        a man who could kill with words.

She left Greenbush as Fire
    Flower, Sparkling Fire, & Ish-
        scoodah, headed for Oberlin

College at thirteen,
    the Credit River Reserve
        in her voice, consonants caught

in her throat, her tongue
    lonely for anything Chippewa
        & African, emerging Edmonia

Lewis. She couldn't stop,
    couldn't keep creatures & fish
        out of her head, porcupine

quills & beads woven into her
    footsteps lost in distant grass,
        & called herself Wildfire

in the gaze of blue eyes.
    She worked light into paper
        up in a second-floor room,

a pencil unearthing *Urania*
    as a marriage gift for Clara,
        her classmate. But nothing

overshadowed the two girls
    who swore she doctored
        their wine with Spanish fly

before two boys took them
    sledding. Attackers left her for dead
        in the snow. She was still thankful

for John Langston,
    a godsend who could argue
        vomitus & urine in court—corpus

delicti. A yellow bird
    clung to a low branch
        as shadows fell asleep

against a stony slab.
    She drew night & day,
        but when someone claimed

she stole a gilded frame
    to hold a Neoclassical picture
        in her head, she departed

for Boston. To Florence,
    to Rome, to her own Way
        of the Cross, till she could see

her brother, Sunrise, digging
    for gold out in California,
        till the sea-green distance

made her lonelier than white
    marble begging for a mallet.
        She could still hear that

chapel bell clanging
    after they hanged John
        Brown, as the chisel

cut curves, her mind
    into the stone: *Hygieia,*
        The Old Indian Arrowmaker

& His Daughter, Asleep,
    Awake, & Forever Free
        rose out of shook blood

& myth. "I thought
    I knew everything when
        I came to Rome, but I found

I had everything to learn."
    As if to make the lowest rock
        forgive itself for lightness,

she couldn't stop carving
    Hagar's face into it: Egyptian
        handmaiden driven out to wander,

bearing her master's child.
    Could she capture the hour
        her family was banned

from the Mississauga
    because night owned their faces?
        Too many whirling paths

brought her to "the day
    Pope Pius IX blessed"
        the figure she was working on,

vespers of remembered fields
    at her feet. Giving herself
        to its heft, she drove away

loneliness with each blow.
    Where did she disappear
        like fireweed approaching

snow? In the mid-1970s,
    in the midst of another long, hot
        summer, a fireman found

The Death of Cleopatra
    among cranes & clamshell buckets,
        & he couldn't stop saying,

"The most beautiful thing . . .
    a big white ghost." So,
        this is how she ended up

after "Blind John" Condon,
    a Chicago gambler & fixer
        who owned a racetrack,

placed her on the grave
    of his favorite horse
        till the pine leaf yellows,

till *Cupid Caught*
    no longer mouths
        the sculptor's last song.

The leaves are outrageously
   crimson here. *Carnaval*
      is in my head, & Robert

Schumann calls for Clara.
   Am I really in Düsseldorf?
      Thinking of *The saint*

of the inner light,
   I see brownshirts
      searching Paul Klee's

house, confiscating love
   letters to his wife
      Lily. Everything begs

remembrance. Tributes
   to the worms at work
      come alive again,

ready to harvest
   the stunned leap year
      as doubt invades sap

& root. Can *Entartete*
   Kunst & *Malkasten* fit
      into the same mouth?

Vandyke Brown, Terre Verte,
   Indian Red, Madder Lake
      & a trifle of Burnt Sienna

to paint a black face.
  Words divide flesh
    into the garden.

The Paint-Box artists
  color in Adam & Eve,
    using every hue & cry

of temptation. Because God
  blends into the darkness
    the faces keep coming off.

Someone lightly brushed the penis
   alive. Belief is almost
      flesh. Wings beat,

dust trying to breathe, as if the figure
   might rise from the oils
      & flee the dead

artist's studio. For years
   this piece of work was there
      like a golden struggle

shadowing Thomas McKeller, a black
   elevator operator at the Boston
      Copley Plaza Hotel, a friend

of John Singer Sargent—hidden
   among sketches & drawings, a model
      for Apollo & a bas-relief

of Arion. So much taken
   for granted & denied, only
      grace & mutability

can complete this face belonging
   to Greek bodies castrated
      with a veil of dust.

They're on the edge
  of their seats, nodding
    heads up & down.

You know how the devil
  tortures the soul?
    He keeps them waiting.

Fat meat . . . Broadnax's wife
  steps out of the grandfather clock
    for the seventeenth time

& throws herself into Trueblood's arms.
  The bedroom fills with feathers
    again. He's Caliban,

savoring the punishment
  of their eyes like the last
    drops of a strong drink.

Yellow jackets blooming on a jaybird—
  this always grabs their minds. Yes,
    now, nothing can stop Zeus

in the astonishment of falling
  feathers. The dream woman's
    forbidden scent is deep

as his own. He craves
  the hex & lash, but his enemies
    reward his downfall with time,

cash, & plugs of tobacco.
    Norton, the philanthropist,
        meditates on his daughter

till she stands nude
    before him. He peels open a red
        Moroccan-leather wallet

& extracts a hundred-dollar bill,
    erecting his monument
        to someone "more delicate

than the wildest dream
    of a poet." Standing
        beside the sharecropper,

he pays for the look in her eyes
    before she started to fade
        in those ice-capped

Alps. But each sunrise
    the same question begs
        the wound raw again.

Dear Mr. Satchmo,
   I'm on the other side
      with "Tiger Rag" & "Way Down

Yonder in New Orleans"
   on the turntable, a heart
      drawn on the soles of my feet.

Here, in the inner sanctum,
   I see you toting buckets of coal
      to Storyville's red-light houses.

You are a small figure
   raising a pistol to fire
      at God in the night sky,

but when I turn to look
   out at the evening star
      your face is mine. You

are holding a bugle
   in your first cutting contest
      with fate. From back o'

town to the Sphinx
   & Buckingham Palace,
      to the Cotton Club

& soccer fields in Africa, under
   spotlights with Ella & Billie
      one hundred nighttimes sweated up

from Congo Square. Listening
    to your notes across the river,
        the sea across miles of salt

trees, I hear a birth
    holler pushing through brass
        at the Lincoln Gardens

in '22 with Papa Joe,
    the Hot Five,
        the Hot Seven . . .

the sun on your horn
    makes me think this note
        can find you, Satchmo.

The Singing Brakeman
    beckoned you to Culver City
        to cut your deep light

into wax, & Miss Lil
    followed, trying to sew up
        a ragged seam. When you blow

I feel like you're talking
    to me, talking about Mayann
        & Mama Lucy as if

they're the same person—
    Lucille dancing on the edge
        of the stage—a loved one

selling fish in the Third Ward.
    In a corner of the naked
        eye, your smile isn't

a smile: confessions & curses
    drip from your trumpet,
        & notes about the FBI

dogging your footsteps
    since '48, float like ghosts
        of reefer smoke in an alley.

Ike wanted you to change
    your words about Little Rock
        as you wove hex signs

into "Indiana" & "Sleepy
    Down South." By the time
        the bomb in Memphis

settled into your mind,
    you were already back
        in Corona blowing triplets

for three or four boys
    sitting on your front steps.
        If you & your drummer

couldn't play on the same stage,
    New Orleans was only a bronze statue
        in a park. Satchmo, I believe

in your horn, how it takes us
    to a woman standing in a cane field
        circled with peacocks.

Yes, I say, I know
   what you mean.
      Then we're off

improvising on what
   ifs: can you imagine
      Langston & Lorca

hypnotized at a window
   in Nella Larsen's
      apartment, pointing at

bridges & searchlights
   in a summer sky, can you
      see them? Their iced breaths

circle a windowpane,
   & one puffed cloud is
      the same as the other.

They click their glasses
   of Jamaican rum. *To your*
      great king, says Lorca.

Prisoner in a janitor's suit,
   adds Langston. Their laughter
      ferries them to a side street

in the Alhambra,
   & at that moment
      they see old Chorrojumo,

King of the Gypsies,
   clapping his hands
      & stamping his feet

along with a tall woman
   dancing a rhumba to a tom-tom's
      moan. Is this Florence

Mills, or another face
   from the Cotton Club
      almost too handsome

to look at? To keep
   a dream of Andalusian
      cante jondo alive.

They agree to meet
   at Small's Paradise
      the next night, where

the bells of trumpets
   breathe honeysuckle & reefer,
      where women & men make love

to the air. You can see
   them now, reclining
      into the Jazz

Age. You can hear Lorca
   saying he cured his fear
      of falling from the SS *Olympic*

by dreaming he was shot
   three times in the head
      near the Fuente Grande

on the road to Alfacar.
   But the word *sex* doesn't
      flower in that heat wave

of 1929, only one man touching
   the other's sleeve, & heads
      swaying to "Beale Street Blues."

Her bedroom's decorated with faces
  of Rudy Vallee, Ginger Rogers
    & Princess Margaret Rose.

A shock of brightness
  pushes me into a room of white
    banners & swastikas unfurled

like a field blooming smoke.
  I face a gelatinous photo
    of pale children running

hands over a black man's
  head. They aren't rubbing
    his kinky hair for luck,

or gazing into a make-believe
  crystal ball to measure
    themselves against mystery.

When touching their own
  hair, did they trace
    from crown to nape,

to the meaning of death?
  If they were now here,
    would their fingers

strain not to touch my head
  as I glimpse a battalion
    of multicolored tulips

watching yellow stars
  slip into this house
    anywhere they could?

If harm hid underneath
  floorboards, inside walls,
    it couldn't touch her.

As she grew, her height
  was marked on a door
    like calibrations for a mortar.

After the phrenology
  of passion fruit & apples
    in The Garden, a good

year before stealing
  into her hiding place,
    before the moon untied

blood, she lingered there
  on the edge of ascension,
    surrendering to a blond boy's kiss.

TO BEAUTY

Just painting things black
will get you nowhere.

—OTTO DIX

The jazz drummer's
   midnight skin
      balances the whole

room, the American
   flag dangling from his breast
      pocket. An album

cover. "Everything
   I have ever seen is
      beautiful." A decade

before a caricaturist
   draws a Star of David
      for a saxophonist's lapel

on the poster of *Jonny*
   spielt auf, Dix's brush
      played every note & shade

of incarnadine darkness.
   Here's his self-portrait
      with telephone, as if

clutching a mike
   like Frank Sinatra—
      posed as an underworld

character, or poised
    for a dance step.
        Shimmy & Charleston,

perfumed & cocksure.
    You'd never know
        he sat for hours

darning his trousers
    with a silver needle,
        stitching night shadows

to facade. The rosy lady's
    orange hair & corsage
        light up the dance floor,

all their faces stopped
    with tempera & time.
        The drummer's shirt

the same hue & texture
    as a woman's dress,
        balanced on the edge

of some anticipated
    embrace. The yellow
        feathers of a rare bird

quiver in a dancer's hat,
    past the drumskin tattooed
        with an Indian chief.

The dark-skinned man corralled
   you into a triangle of trees
      & barbed wire, the two

of you swaying on horseback,
   twilight catching a knife.
      He was already dead

in the saddle when
   his spooked palomino
      broke & ran. You

were my grandmother's second
   husband, with your cheap
      wine & Lucky Strikes,

your two hunting dogs
   with that nightmare
      you couldn't corner

even with the Delta
   blues. I didn't know
      what they meant by "Red's

got a white man's job"
   as you measured lumber
      & jotted numbers on a pad.

If I held your drunken
   portrait beside
      Walter White's

or President Harding's
  yours would be paler,
    more blond. One gray eye,

one blue. You never
  spent a day in jail.
    No wonder you believed

in ghosts. Like a man
  who eats red onions
    to cry, you'd get drunk

& start talking about
  how they found the horse
    grazing on bitter goldenrod

beside a creek, its rider
  purple as an eggplant, his left foot
    still tangled in the stirrup.

TWILIGHT SEDUCTION

Because Duke's voice
    was smooth as new silk
        edged with Victorian lace, smooth

as Madam Zajj nude
    beneath her mink coat,
        I can't help but run

my hands over you at dusk.
    Hip to collarbone, right ear-
        lobe to the sublime. Simply

because Jimmy Blanton
    died at twenty-one
        & his hands on the bass

still make me ashamed
    to hold you like an upright
        & a cross worked into one

embrace. Fingers pulse
    at a gold zipper, before
        the brain dances the body

into a field of poppies.
    Duke knew how to listen
        to colors, for each sigh shaped

out of sweat & blame,
    knew a Harlem air shaft
        could recall the whole

night in an echo: prayers,
    dogs barking, curses & blessings.
        Plunger mute tempered

by need & plea. He'd search
    for a flaw, a small scar
        some mark of perfect

difference for his canvas.
    I hold your red shoes,
        one in each hand to balance

the sky, because Duke
    loved Toulouse-Lautrec's
        nightlife. Faces of women

woven into chords scribbled
    on hotel stationery—blues,
        but never that unlucky

green. April 29th
    is also my birthday,
        the suspicious wishbone

snapped between us,
    & I think I know why
        a pretty woman always

lingered *at the bass*
    clef end of the piano.
        Tricky Sam coaxed

an accented wa-wa
   from his trombone, coupled
      with Cootie & Bubber,

& Duke said, *Rufus,*
   give me some ching-chang
      & sticks on the wood.

I tell myself the drum
   can never be a woman,
      even if her name's whispered

across skin. Because
   nights at the Cotton Club
      shook on the bone,

because Paul Whiteman
   sat waiting for a riff
      he could walk away with

as feathers twirled
   among palm trees, because
      Duke created something good

& strong out of thirty pieces
   of silver like a spotlight
      on conked hair,

because so much flesh
   is left in each song,
      because women touch

themselves to know
   where music comes from,
      my fingers trace

your lips to open up
   the sky & let in
      the night.

HOMAGE TO A BELLHOP

*. . . it startled us no more
than a blue vase or a red rug.*
—RICHARD WRIGHT, *BLACK BOY*

Looks that weren't
   looks, like dazed
      swimmers gazing up

through twenty feet
   of untroubled water,
      you flexed your brimming

strength, a naked mask
   rehearsal. Because
      of unspoken treaties between

shadows & antebellum
   porticoes, between you
      & a prostitute, the third

face in the room was always
   erased from such a burlesque.
      You tipped your bright top hat

for every half dollar
   palmed into your callused
      hands. The small secrets

multiplied till they pulled
   you toward aquamarine waves
      & hills, or down in the basement

with the shoeshine boy,
   reading *Flash Gordon*
      & dime store novels

till the next buzzer
   summoned you up.
      Familiar with the sounds

of each slurred blue note
   & faked orgasm, you
      fixed your face before

that old soft knock
   on the door. Passion fruit
      quartered on a crystal dish

red as forbidden lips.
   You didn't see the woman
      on the bed, tied to the man

by a string of pearls.
   How many bets did they lose
      trying to make you betray

your daughter at Fisk?
   But you were a stone
      beside a river, a tiger

fashioned into a pussycat.
   Even later, in the deep nights,
      you couldn't escape

them—when you crawled
  into bed to make love
    to your wife, their hands

would rest on the dampened sheet
  & their sighs would pool
    into your inner ear.

Ralph Ellison didn't
    have his right hand
        on her left breast

& they weren't kissing
    in the doorway of Blackmur's
        kitchen. But Delmore

Schwartz tried to slap
    his wife, Elizabeth,
        at the Christmas party

anyway. When he pulled
    her into a side bedroom
        the house swelled into a big

white amp for Caliban's
    blues. Maybe their fight
        began one evening about sex

years earlier, not enough
    money for food & gasoline.
        But she'd only been leaning

against Ellison's shoulder
    to let him light her cigarette,
        just a lull in a conversation

about Duke Ellington's
    "Creole Love Call"
        & the New Critics.

That night, the falling
    snow through the windows
        was a white spotlight

on his dark face,
    a perfect backdrop
        for Delmore's rehearsal

for the women
    who would pass
        through his life

like stunned llamas,
    for the drunken stars
        exploding in his head,

for the taxicabs
    taken from Cambridge
        to Greenwich Village, the fear

of death, the Dexedrine
    clouds & poison-pen letters
        floating back to earth,

for the notes in the margins
    of Rilke's *Duino*
        Elegies & his love-hate

of T. S. Eliot,
    for Chumley's Bar,
        those days of gray

boxcars flickering past
   as he paced Washington
      Square Park, impulsive

bouquets stolen from gardens
   & given to lovers with dirt
      clinging to the roots,

for his fascination
   with Marilyn Monroe,
      the Dreyfus case, Kafka

quoting Flaubert, the day
   after JFK's assassination
      spent wandering the streets

in unbuckled galoshes,
   for Cavanaugh's Irish Bar
      in Chelsea & the Egyptian

Gardens on West Twenty-ninth,
   Dixie's Plantation Lounge,
      for his last night on earth,

stumbling from a forest
   of crumpled girlie magazines,
      as he takes the garbage

down to the lobby,
   singing about lovers
      in the Duchess's red shoes.

Sierva María do
    Todos los Ángeles,
        red-haired Igbo,

the senses eat us
    to the rind. I wake,
        still holding *Of Love*

& Other Demons,
    with Bartolomé de
        Las Casas in the room

again. He's talking
    about how Africans
        worship sun-gods

& can endure the cat-o'-
    nine-tails with less
        blood on the grass,

about Indians killing
    themselves. His Latin
        tamed the rapacious

mastiff & peregrine
    & drew in villagers
        on shattered kneecaps.

I know he's in the thick
    fragrance of mock orange
        & human sweat. Sugar

& salvation mixed
    into a lethean mist
        that hid Hispaniola

in logbooks of white
    pages, as sailors
        dismantled ships

& built forts. After
    they were raped, the women
        begged sacred trees

& stones to kill
    curses hidden inside. Plumed
        in his scarlet cassock,

the Apostle of the Indies
    stood in for Satan's
        timekeeper, overseeing

fields of yam & cassava.
    Why did he say the poets
        had to forgive him before

his feet could take root?
    He closed his salty eyes
        & blessed the seamen

who first glimpsed
    the bright earrings
        when the Arawaks

swam out to greet
    the Spanish galleon,
        before gifts of feathers

& cotton, as the sun
    struck their little
        gold death notes.

She flushes barbiturates
  down the toilet, before
    returning to a pyramid

of books stacked on pale satin
  sheets, wearing only a bra.
    She's Norma Jean,

Marilyn, & now thinks of Abe
  Lincoln & Albert Einstein
    again, wondering if

there's an afterlife.
  What did they believe?
    She remembers Carl

Sandburg's openmouthed
  gaze as she recited by heart
    the *Gettysburg Address,*

that she said *Gemini*
  to answer him. He shifted
    his feet when she asked

about the riots on beaches
  in Chicago. Did he talk
    with Yeats at Harriet Monroe's

banquet, & what did he
  mean about Abyssinians,
    Zulus, & Bushmen?

She could still hear
   herself reciting "Never
      Give All the Heart,"

can see him turn away
   from her when she said
      if King ever marched

to the Lincoln Memorial
   she'd be there, that
      Harry Belafonte

lives between dreams. Yes,
   Sandburg dissolves like "bees'
      wings in a late summer sun"

when her eyelashes record
   an unspoken loneliness
      beneath dust & holy

water, unable to stop
   hands running down the full
      length of her body.

I am not in Miami
    when I hear Mongo
        Santamaria's bloodstained

fingers ripple the conga
    skins stretched over myth
        & curved wood. Oricha,

santos, & the old gods
    of revenge & sacrifice
        are in a strange land.

I am with Langston
    Hughes at Las Villas
        Inn at 20 Avenida

Belgica—night & day
    mix into the lexicon
        of names & streets:

a Cuban dinner
    at Café El Paradiso,
        demitasse & Benedictine.

A forest of gourds, guitars,
    rattles, trumpets, Japanese
        lanterns & streamers, flutes

holding stars in focus
    as Lalita Zamora opens
        a rose with her smile

& spices glow inside
    darkness. Club Atenas
        & Club Occidente—

claves, guavos racas,
    keys to the *son's* call
        & response. I am

not in Miami, not close
    to the Florida Everglades
        where Seminoles rise

out of sweetgrass.
    Or some other life
        where a train conductor

& passengers shout, "Leave
    him alone. He's the great
        artiste, Brindis de Sala."

I am not in Miami.
    Chango's thunderbolts
        strike thieves & conjurers

of bad magic. The Venus
    Ochun swims the River
        Oshun. "Yo quisiera

ser Negro. Bien Negro.
    ¡Negro de verdad!"
        I am sitting between

Langston & Nicholás
 Guillén, as car lights
  flicker on the water

outside Marianao. Blues
 fill our mouths like ripe
  jackfruit, & when Mongo

touches the drumhead
 we are one hundred years
  from the greenbacks

glistening with the sweat
 of blacks who work sugar.
  His fingers are taped

like the Bolo Kid's,
 as if his big hands
  were made for machetes

in a land where days
 are fast as bright dresses
  on the edge of maroon

hills, & where midnight
 drums shake loose gilded
  nails in a racketeer's coffin.

OIL

Now, when I hear Horace
    Silver's "Baghdad Blues"
        the sandy sky blooms

smart bombs. Live
    footage of an old man
        on a yellow bicycle

trying to outpedal
    the apocalypse—
        the film runs till

he's my uncle Buddy
    who turned to mist
        after his father hocked

two hundred acres to go
    his bail. He'd killed a man
        who cornered him in Biloxi.

I am surprised to see
    my grandmother's twin
        riding out of war fog.

I can still hear her
    saying, "Ku Klux
        & two birds with one

stone." Silver's piano
    pulses beneath the burning
        oil fields, the volume

turned down on the tv
    till the ghost of At-
        Thinnin (The Dragon),

Caliph of Baghdad,
    floats through smoke.
        My grandmother's voice

says, "Son, you don't
    know how it hurt us to see
        those oil wells bowing

& rising like big birds
    eating my father's farm."
        In her faded print dress,

she's in a pavilion
    of eunuchs, lions, & peacocks,
        beside the Caliph's mother,

Shakla. This man of disguises
    who wandered Baghdad streets,
        as eater of fish tongues,

who wove a war anthem
    against King Theophilus,
        couldn't burn love songs

on his deathbed: "Fool
    thou art, what should I do
        with beloved Charayah?

Ought I to burn her too?
    She knows all my songs
        by heart." Like a film

of sleep, oil covers camera
    lenses & the old man's face
        as he rides into the flames.

So, this is where
    cries come to us,
        where molting seagulls

peck the air. I never
    thought Crown Heights
        would be so quiet, just

a cantor & a blues singer
    weaving all the old begats
        into Cato, Yankel, Andy,

Michael, James . . . all the others
    transplanted to earthen dams
        & tenements. Sabbath-breakers

& charlatans sow seeds to kill
    fruit. What we forgot
        or never knew is enough

to teach the ant to profane
    sugar. To see injustice,
        don't care where your feet

are planted, you must be
    able to nail your left hand
        to a tree in full bloom.

Now, look at Sheba
    in Solomon's hanging garden,
        carved by grace from head

to toe, she was "wounded
　　by love of wisdom" hidden
　　　　in a cloud of galbanum

& myrrh. Didn't the King
　　trust his heart? Let's hope
　　　　the crystal floor

over that silent stream
　　had nothing to do with
　　　　the color of her skin,

but to prove her legs
　　weren't like a donkey's.
　　　　We sense what we've done

even if we can't say why
　　we're dismayed or overjoyed
　　　　by how the stones fit

in our hands. The egg
　　& sperm we would love
　　　　to deny, they still move

the blood till we can hear,
　　"I am black but comely,
　　　　ye daughters of Jerusalem."

Some of us grow ashamed
　　peering up from the rat's hole
　　　　in the belly of the Ark

till we're no longer the same
    women & men. Like Sheba
        & Solomon, who asked

hard questions, we know
    if a man is only paid
        a stud fee,

he'll butt his head
    till stars rain down
        & kill some stranger.

She eyes my haircut
    & jeans with the blue
        washed out. A pink

bubble detonates in her mouth quick
    as a July maypop, & she flips
        her pressed hair like Lauren

Bacall in *The Big Sleep.*
    No, I won't do my best
        imitation of Bogart. I am

thinking about Hatshepsitu
    who wrestled gods & bloodlines
        in the Valley of the Kings,

light-years ahead of this coed
    gazing into her compact
        mirror, with a hint

of stereophonic Fishbone
    escaping from the headphones
        of her Sony Walkman.

I'm not upwardly mobile enough,
    am I? Her texts are sealed
        in their prophylactic

covers, *The Deconstruction
of Hannibal Lecter* about
        to fall from her book bag.

Hatshepsitu's obelisks
    blocked the midday sun
        from the temple of Amen-Ra.

She donned a man's garb
    & changed her name to Hatshepsut,
        after declaring God seduced her

mother "in a flood of light
    & perfume." The oil of ani
        scented her limbs

till her fragrance reached
    the land of Punt.
        Lost in her mirror

again, waiting to pay
    a twenty-five-dollar
        overdraft, this coed

stands as if she were at Deir
    el-Bahari in a temple. But sex
        goes out of me. It gives up

like an angel lying down within,
    since there's so little of herself
        she's learned to praise.

As if the night
  on Fire Island
    never happened—the dune

buggy that cut
  like a scythe of moonlight
    across the sand—I see

Frank O'Hara
  with Mapplethorpe's
    book of photographs.

He whistles "Lover
  Man" beneath his breath,
    nudging that fearful

40th year into the background,
  behind those white waves
    of sand. A quick

lunch at Moriarty's
  with someone called LeRoi,
    one of sixty best friends

in the city. He's hurting
  to weigh Melville's concept
    of evil against Henry

James. That woman begging
  a nickel has multiplied
    one hundredfold since

he last walked past the House
   of Seagram. They speak
      of Miles Davis

clubbed twelve times
   outside Birdland by a cop,
      & Frank flips through pages

of Mapplethorpe as if searching
   for something to illustrate
      the cop's real fear.

A dog for the exotic—
   is this what he meant?
      The word Nubian

takes me to monuments
   in Upper Egypt, not
      the "kiss of birds

at the end of the penis"
   singing in the heart
      of America. Julie Harris

merges with images of Bob Love
   till *East of Eden* is
      a compendium of light

& dark. Is this O'Hara's
   Negritude? The phallic temple
      throbs like someone

breathing on calla lilies
  to open them: Leda's
    room of startled mouths.

NETHERWORLDS

The day hurts. Each leaf
   scribbles crimsoned ocher
      across the lousy silence.

Chocolate cherries
   wrapped in silver foil
      make my fillings ache.

I'm pulled down to the bed.
   Pages flip. Late October,
      1989. Yes, I think

I know this house where
   an off-duty cop says
      You must be Robert

Lowell. That's in another city,
   & please don't ask why I'm here
      standing before this bronze heft

as the 54th marches past mansions
   & clubs with drawn windowshades.
      One hundred threadbare boots

climb the sandy hills
   of Fort Wagner, their gold cross
      on a star still up there.

Maybe a few minutes
   of the evening news,
      & then a light dinner

downstairs. Something hot
   & spicy. What's this?
      No. A black man

did what, shot a pregnant
   woman? The whole city
      hurts. A skeleton key

shines like gunmetal
   on the floor of the Charles
      River. I count roses

on the wallpaper till night
   turns into snapdragons
      around a pale casket.

I bet this is how Lowell felt
   next to that crook Lepke.
      I'm afraid to go out

into those Boston streets:
   so many netherworlds drift
      through each other,

dividing like cells.
   The cops blackjack
      the night till it confesses.

Stars on the ground
   finger the woman's jewelry
      & the gun in a paper bag.

The evidence pulls me back
    into myself. In Dunbarton
      I'm in another country

of Christmas snow, across
    from the old farmhouse.
      The two faces holding

the picture in focus, who
    knew your mother & father
      when they were alive,

can you hurt them
    with love? I hear you
      say, *He's only a friend.*

I stand beneath petals
    falling from wallpaper.
      We have our arms around

each other, gazing over
    a wrought-iron fence
      at Lowell's grave.

A grackle & red bird
    flit among icy sumac
      branches, shaking berries

till they're like silent
    bullet holes in the lily-
      white funereal air,

& I wonder if his ghost
    is angry at our bodies
        aflame under the trees.

Those double shotgun
   houses in New Orleans
      can get a man killed.

Helena suns in our shared
   courtyard in her crimson
      swimsuit. Her breasts

point toward my back
   door, just mesh & light
      between us. I want to

talk about friendship,
   about how an August day's
      brightness can murder.

She lies against the ground,
   moving her hips to the music,
      reading Joaquim Machado

de Assis again. Whispered
   Portuguese floats to me
      through magnolia scent.

We listen to Afro-Cuban
   because we both can move
      to the drum. Her husband

is draped in computer cables
   somewhere. I want to say
      that de Assis's skin color

didn't have anything to do
   with indelible printing ink
      on his hands, that "Mosca

Azul" & "Circulo Viciosi"
   had been woven into one
      unbroken song of colors

in my head. The blue
   fly's "wings of gold
      & Carmine" were also

the glowworm's lament
   about the sky, the sun's
      wish to be a glowworm.

I want to tell her how
   she's wounded me with
      red cloth, but before

I can walk across the room
   a ghost or guardian angel
      slams the door shut.

We're on our knees
  in his backyard
    like two boys shooting

marbles, as he draws
  circles & X's mysterious
    as hex signs in the dirt.

I tell him Hannibal's
  war tactics don't excite me,
    but he's somewhere else

in his hierarchy of phalanxes
  & battlements. Now, he scribbles
    Othello & quickly erases

it with his hands,
  & says, "Love & jealousy
    filled his mouth with poetry

& killed him." He looks at me
  & grins. "But Othello's
    only fictional," I say.

"No, he's actually
  a composite," the archivist
    says. Then he writes

Masinissa in the dirt
  & underlines it. "Now,
    it was love that made him

into a great warrior.
    Did you ever see *Cabiria*,
        that Italian movie?"

I shake my head.
    "At seventeen, he came to study
        tactics & Latin in Carthage,

& fell for Sophonisba.
    They say she was so pretty
        she could melt a stone

charm if a man held it
    on his tongue. He was a boy
        in a man's body

when he goaded her father,
    Hasdrubal, to declare war
        on Syphax, so he could fight

& prove himself in battle
    to win Sophonisba's love.
        Syphax was defeated in two battles."

He punches me twice
    on the arm, & then something
        makes me laugh: I see

my boyhood friend, Bill,
    rigging the rifle, before
        he runs through the trap

to show how it worked
   in the movie, before the bullet
      sinks into his thigh.

"What's funny—I mean,
   this is for real. Masinissa
      wasn't even eighteen

when he went to Spain
   with Hasdrubal & attacked
      Scipio, Rome's greatest general

& defeated him. But Syphax
   locked in & allied the Romans
      & threatened Carthage

till Sophonisba married
   him." His bald head
      is aimed at me,

& I'm thinking how
   his two daughters danced
      the grass down in a circle

in the middle of the yard
   where we're on our knees
      with their jump ropes

& endless cartwheels.
   "Are you with me?
      After Masinissa heard

the news in Spain,
   he went to Hasdrubal
      who sided with Syphax,

& it was then he secretly
   joined the Romans before
      heading home to Massylia

a small kingdom in southern
   Numida. It wasn't long
      before Syphax attacked.

Badly wounded,
   Masinissa hid in a cave
      with the five men left,

& false mourners
   chanted songs of his death
      till Scipio marched into Africa

to join him. Outnumbered,
   he then sent a peace note,
      & then sneaked into the camp

of the Numidians & set it
   afire." The archivist's eyes
      steal a few sparks

from the air. The two
   sculpted glasses half-
      filled with rum summon us

like abandoned chess pieces
   on the tiled squares
      of the patio. "Man,

the Numidians thought
   the fire was an accident,
      so they ran out without

weapons. Do I need
   to say any more? The same
      happened to the Carthaginians—

their camp ablaze,
   forty thousand dead
      & a thousand top-notch

horses & four elephants
   captured, Hasdrubal
      & Syphax tried to hide

behind the city walls.
   Syphax said it wasn't
      arms that beat him, so he

raised another army
   from the dust & attacked.
      This time, Masinissa

beat him toe-to-toe,
   wrestled him into chains
      and marched him to Cirta,

where Sophonisba waited
  with her maidens. She
    threw herself down

at his feet & begged
  him to kill her,
    saying, 'Let death

take me rather than
  a Roman under the skies
    of Africa.' Of course,

he married her before
  Lelius & Scipio
    marched into the city."

I say, "I don't want blood
  on the hands of my heroes."
    Our eyes meet & we hold

the stare of green-eyed
  cats that go all the way
    back to Egypt. He says,

"You want perfection
  without the salt. Angels
    without birthmarks."

The way the sun falls
  in the doorway, I can't
    tell if it's my wife,

his wife, or his daughter
Louise, beckoning us
to come in for dinner.

Rape & *pillage* are the two
words on my tongue. I stand up
& brush the dust off my hands.

"Syphax didn't give up.
He said to Lelius:
'I was ruined.

But I have one consolation.
Sophonisba has passed
into the hands of my enemy

who has shown himself
no wiser than I.' Now,
Scipio heard this from Lelius,

& he sent for Masinissa
& said to him: 'Do not
tarnish your virtues

by a single vice.'
OK, now let's go in
& have some food."

The archivist stands up
& brushes his hands
on his trousers, smiling.

He's aced me again,
  like a lover getting up
    in the middle of sex

to answer a phone call
  halfway around the world.
    The ringing in my head,

the questions that won't
  stop. Again & again,
    I return for this battle

royal on Saturdays.
  I wondered what he'd do
    if I hugged him.

The swastika tattooed
  on his right bicep & a nude
  on his left quiver-dance

as he tries to blowtorch
  St. Maurice of Aganaum
  off Saxony's coat-of-

arms. When the flame
  spits a molten bead
  of blue on his steel-toed

boots, obscenities
  leap into the bruised
  night. Since his buddy

Awesome chickened out,
  he wonders if the picture
  in the Alte Pinakothek

would have been easier.
  Now that he's started,
  where does he stop,

does he go to Coburg,
  Cracow, the Cathedral
  of Lucerne, Schwarzkopf

in Riga, the cloth makers
  & dyers, the tomb of Archbishop
  Ernest at Magdeburg, where

next? He hums a verse
　　from Bone Thugs & Harmony,
　　　　punching the air as if to break

the saint's armor. Well,
　　his ex-girlfriend, Blanche,
　　　　she would know what to do,

how to calm him down
　　when he begins to whimper
　　　　& cut initials into his skin.

"Can you spare seven cents?"
    I drop two quarters into
        his McDonald's cup,

& he runs after me, saying,
    "Man, I can't take this.
        I don't want to get rich."

I notice the 1st Cav. patch
    on his fatigue jacket. He smells
        like he slept in a field of mint.

He says that he's Benedict
    the Moor. Of course, I've
        never heard of the fellow.

Two days later, I spot him
    outside Cody's Bookstore
        & reach into my pocket,

fingering the pennies. He says,
    "I'm not begging today, brother.
        I'm just paying penance."

He goes back to scrubbing
    the sidewalk with a wire brush.
        His black & white mutt

stands there; she guards him
    at night while he sleeps
        under a crown of stars.

I find what I'm looking for
  at the Berkeley library.
    He was born in Sicily

on the estate of Chevalier de
  Lanza of San Fratello,
    the son of African slaves.

He sold the lumbering oxen
  he'd labored years to buy,
    gave the money to the poor,

& followed Father Lanza, pledging
  a Lenten vow. After the caves
    in the mountains near Palermo,

he went to live in a rocky cell
  on Monte Pellegrino where
    the Duke of Medina-Coeli

visited & built him a chapel.
  All the titles at his feet
    Benedict the Moor

rejected. He couldn't
  read or write, but recited
    biblical passages for days.

Wearing just a few leaves,
  he predicted the death
    of Princess Bianca,

made the sign of the cross
　　to win the blind sight. Here
　　　　was a man who hid in a thicket

from a crowd's joy.
　　The Duchess of Montalvo
　　　　bowed often before him,

but she never saw his eyes.
　　"Into thy hands, O Lord,
　　　　I commend my spirit"

were his last words. Three months
　　later, I sit in the Blue Nile
　　　　eating with my hands, folding

pieces of spicy chicken
　　into spongy white bread
　　　　thin as forgiveness,

knowing that one hand
　　is sacred & the other used
　　　　to clean oneself with leaves

or clutch a dagger. No one
　　touched Benedict the Moor's
　　　　hands. Not even the Duchess.

They kissed the hem of his habit.
　　In Palermo, the senate burned
　　　　fourteen torches of white wax

in his honor. When I step out
   under Berkeley's cool stars,
      I see the face I thought

lost in the Oakland hills
   when eucalyptus created
      an inferno. I walk up

to him, fingering a nickel
   & two pennies. He says,
      "Can you spare three cents?"